PRIEST AND LAYMAN

A. DONDEYNE

PRIEST AND LAYMAN

translated by

N. D. SMITH

SHEED AND WARD
LONDON AND NEW YORK

FIRST PUBLISHED 1964
SHEED AND WARD LTD
33 MAIDEN LANE
LONDON W.C.2
AND
SHEED AND WARD INC
64 UNIVERSITY PLACE
NEW YORK 3

NIHIL OBSTAT: JOANNES M. T. BARTON, S.T.D., L.S.S.
CENSOR DEPUTATUS

IMPRIMATUR: ✠ GEORGIUS L. CRAVEN,
EPÚS SEBASTOPOLIS VIC. GEN.

WESTMONASTERII, DIE 9A APRILIS 1964

The Nihil obstat and Imprimatur are a declaration that a book or pamphlet is considered to be free from doctrinal or moral error. It is not implied that those who have granted the Nihil obstat and Imprimatur agree with the contents, opinions or statements expressed.

Originally published as *Priester en leek*, Antwerp, Uitgeverij Patmos (1962).

This book is set in 12 pt. Linotype Baskerville

Made and printed in Great Britain by William Clowes and Sons, Limited, London and Beccles

CONTENTS

INTRODUCTION

THIS short study is directly connected with a more comprehensive work which was published recently under the title of *Geloof en Wereld*.[1]

My aim in *Geloof en Wereld* was to define the nature of the relationship between Christianity and the present world. The principal question was this: Is our presence in the world effective enough? Do we perhaps not live too much side by side with the world, in an enclosed kind of community, more concerned with the preservation and survival of our own group than with the building up of a better world for all men in close association with other men? Does the Church not appear in the eyes of other men as a competitor on the profane level rather than as the bearer of a joyous message which comes from God and is directed to all men?

To be a human being is to be a man among one's fellow men. The Christian is bound,

[1] *Geloof en Wereld* (*The Faith and the World*), Antwerp, Patmos (1961).

more than any other human being, to live as
a man among his fellows, since he is commanded above all to love his neighbour.

A turning-point has been reached in the
history of mankind. Humanity is united. To
help the Christian who is conscious of this
intimate fellowship with his neighbours to
communicate in honest and fruitful dialogue
with other men, to take part in a real human
intercourse, was the principal object and constant theme of *Geloof en Wereld*.

In the present work, I am more concerned
with this communication within the Church
herself, with the dialogue and co-operation
between the Church's priests and her laity,
her hierarchy and those who are subject to
this hierarchy. Throughout, the emphasis is
on what the Bible calls the *aedificatio
Ecclesiae*, the building up of the Church into
what she ought, in God's view, to be: ". . . a
spiritual temple built up of living stones . . . a
kingly priesthood, a holy nation . . . the
people of God". (1 Pet. 2.5–10.) The people
who form the living stones of this Church are
to appear as God's witnesses, as "God's sign
in the midst of the nations". By their faith
and way of life, they are to "declare his
virtues" who has called humanity "out of

darkness into his marvellous light" (1 Pet. 2.9).

This *aedificatio Ecclesiae* can only be the work of the whole of the ecclesiastical community. The Church can only be built up by her priests and her laity together. The three chapters of this book correspond to these three elements.

THE BUILDING UP OF THE CHURCH

WHAT is the Church? What part does she play, and what is her place, in the whole of God's work of salvation?

One of the greatest services which have been rendered by contemporary ecclesiologists, or theologians of the Church, has been to establish a scriptural idea of the Church as the basis and point of departure for all their speculation in this field. This does not mean that our faith in the mystery of the Church, our *Credo sanctam Ecclesiam*, is changed in any way. What has been changed is the manner in which theologians approach this mystery and represent it in their lectures and writings. This change is of the greatest importance, and it is undoubtedly a change for the better in that it enables us to come far more closely into contact with the reality of our faith. Theology is, after all, nothing but a critical examination of the mystery of faith on the part of the believer, whose aim is to reach a better understanding of and to form a more adequate and contemporary idea of the mystery he confesses, and to express it in a way which is more closely adapted to the age in which he is living. Theological speculation, then, is firmly based in faith and is always at the service of faith. Its object is never to replace faith by highflown considerations or complicated conceptualisms, but to bring the mystery of faith closer to us in all its aspects and dimensions and in this way to nourish our life of faith and make it more fruitful by more intimate contact with the realities of salvation. Contemporary theology, and contemporary ecclesiology in particular, has to a very great extent achieved this object of bringing Christians into a much closer and more authentic contact with the living reality of their faith. In this context, then, a brief review of the evolution of ecclesiology over the last fifty years has a direct bearing on our theme.

The Evolution of Ecclesiology

It is not difficult to distinguish three different stages in the evolution of the theology of the Church in the course of the present century.

(1) When the author was himself still a student, attention was directed primarily towards the social and juridical nature of the Church. This emphasis was above all due to a reaction against a certain type of Protestant ecclesiology which tended to place a minimal stress on the visible nature of the Church. The answer given to the question, "What is the Church?" in the Belgian catechism in use before the First World War was: "The assembly of all faithful Christians who confess the lawful teaching of Christ, in obedience to the Pope of Rome." This answer was, in fact, a résumé of the celebrated definition of the Church given by Robert Bellarmine in his *Controversiae Christianae Adversus hujus Temporis Haereticos*. The first part of this appeared in 1586, shortly after the Council of Trent. It read: "The association of those men who are united by their confession of the same Christian faith and their communion in the same sacraments, under the governing authority of the lawful pastors and above all of the one representative of Christ on earth, the Pope of Rome." (*De Eccl.*, 3, no. 2.)

It is clear that the important element in

this definition of the Church was the idea of a "perfect society". In it, the Church was seen first and foremost as a society set up by God and possessing all the characteristics of a perfect society. The greatest emphasis was laid on the visible, hierarchical and juridical character of the Church. It hardly needs to be said that this view of the Church caused the role of the laity and the lay apostolate to remain very much in the background. The laity occupied a subordinate place and, as a subject, the greatest virtue which the layman could have was that of submissiveness.

(2) The most important aspect of the evolution of ecclesiology between the two wars was the growing interest among theologians in the Pauline idea of the mystical body of Christ. This new approach cast a much more favourable light on the supernatural and invisible aspect of the mystery of the Church. At the same time, it revealed the broader basis and the deeper implications of the social and visible character of the Church. It is indeed true to say that far less stress is placed on the juridical aspect of the Church as a social order in the Pauline image of the body of Christ than on the idea of a multiplicity of functions within a single organic unity. All

members of the Church are, according to St Paul, directly connected to the Head, Christ himself, and are moved by the Spirit of the Lord. It is quite obvious, then, that this vision of the Church gave the laity a far wider share in the life of the Church. The layman is, by virtue of his baptism and his faith, a living member of the Church community. What is more, he has no need of any intervening agency in the exercise of his function.

(3) This did not, however, mark the end of the development of Catholic ecclesiology during the present century. A new, and no less important step forward was taken when, after the Second World War, Catholic theology as a whole consciously and noticeably began to adopt a far more biblical approach. Theologians began to gear their studies far more closely to the Old and New Testaments. The word "testament" was, moreover, also seen in its double meaning, that is to say, not only as Holy Scripture, or the collection of sacred books, but also as sacred history, or the history of the divine economy of salvation. This biblical orientation of postwar theology has had extremely favourable consequences for theological thought in general and for ecclesiology in particular. Three concepts

form the basis of all present-day theological thought—the concepts of "grace", "revelation" and "the Word of God". Theologians have, so to speak, gone back to the very origins of these three concepts and have thought them out afresh. Let us consider this question a little more closely.

First and foremost, the concept of grace was approached from a new perspective, that of the history of salvation. The entire subject was thus seen in a fresh light.

We have only to think of the standard writings on grace of the prewar period. In them, grace was defined as a supernatural quality of the soul, infused into the soul by God and enabling man to share in the divine life. It is, of course, true that Christ was regarded as the source of all grace and as the one who had merited all grace by his death on the Cross. Nonetheless, this reference to Christ and his work of salvation was in most cases not included in the essential definitions of grace.

The idea of *charis* (grace) in St Paul, however, at once calls a saving event to mind. This saving event is an act of gracious condescension on God's part, a breakthrough of the divine quality of grace into the history of mankind. The crucifixion and resurrection of the Lord Jesus Christ and the descent of the Holy Ghost are at the very centre of this act—"The goodness and kindness of God, our saviour, appeared", in the words of St Paul, in time. (Titus 3.4.) These qualities became visible in the course of human history in order to bring about our salvation. This very fact established a saving history. The two great periods of the history of man's salvation are the Old and the New Covenant. The Church, as the People of God of the New Covenant, represents the second great period of this history.

Emphasis, then, was placed on the historical aspect of grace. In addition to this, the revelatory character of the supernatural economy of grace came to be seen in a fresh light. The original biblical significance of the concept of "revelation" was restored.

The concept of revelation has always played a prominent part in theology, since theology is, after all, nothing more or less than speculation on the subject of divine revelation ("scientia de Deo et rebus divinis ex revelatione"). In the past, revelation was generally described as a divine proclamation of abstract, supernatural concepts and truths which we accepted in faith and were "bound to know in order to become blessed". This definition of revelation was not incorrect, but it was incomplete. In the Bible, the term "revelation" has a much more concrete meaning. Revelation in the Bible does not, in the first place, refer to abstract concepts and truths concerning God, nor does the Bible aim to proclaim such ideas. On the contrary, the Bible refers to a divine event of salvation, situated within a historical context—the self-revelation of God himself throughout human history and the gradual accomplishment of the promise which God made to Moses: "I will be with thee." (Exod. 3.12.) This divine revelation is divine in two senses—it proceeds from the living God and it has the living God as its object. God, in his self-revelation, emerges from the mystery which conceals him and shows his face to man. Bending over man, God presents himself to him in the first person of the Trinity. Revelation is, thus, synonymous here with "theophany", a divine apparition or a manifestation of God's liberating presence. God reveals himself, in the double sense of making himself known and becoming present, as our saviour and our salvation, as a God who is with us and for us (*nobiscum Deus*).

The incarnation of God's Word—Christ's death and resurrection and the descent of the Holy Ghost which marked the inception of the new People of God, the Church—is, of course, what lies at the very centre of this saving economy of revelation. This central moment of revelation, however, also points towards the ultimate manifestation of the mystery of God's glory and love, to what the Bible calls the "end of time", the ultimate significance and the perfection of history. It is even possible to claim that this time—the last days—has already commenced, since the saving realities of the risen Christ and his sanctifying Spirit are actually present in the world, though still concealed under sacred signs, "until he come", in expectation of the ultimate revelation of the Lord. It is only then that God will make fully manifest to man the exact nature of his relationship with man and of his intentions towards man. In the words which St Paul addressed to the Christian community in Colossae, "You are dead; and your life is hid with Christ in God. When Christ, who is your life, is revealed, then you also shall be revealed with him in glory." (Col. 3.3–4.)

In close conjunction with this reappreciation of the concepts of revelation by present-day theologians is the emergence of a renewed concept, in a strictly biblical sense, of the Word of God. Indeed, contemporary theology is above all a theology of the Word and its proclamation. On the one hand, it is attuned to Johannine thought, according to which our redemption is defined as a work of God's Word, which "was made flesh and dwelt among us". (John 1.14.) On the other hand, it is closely geared to the thought of St Paul, for whom the proclamation of the Christian message in the name of the Lord is never exclusively the work of men, but a "power of God unto salvation of every one that believeth". (Rom. 1.16.)

I have already provided elsewhere a detailed exposition of what is meant by Jesus as the "Word of God".[1] The minimal significance of this concept is that what the human word, in the sense of true human word and not, of course, of mere idle verbiage, is able to accomplish for our positive good in the purely profane sphere of human civilization,

[1] See *Geloof en Wereld,* pp. 43ff.

the Word of God is also able to accomplish in the matter of our divine salvation.

Every true word has a powerfully liberating and revealing effect upon us. Think of the "word" of the poet, the artist, the scientist or the scholar, for example, and how it draws us into the world in which each of these lives and by which each is influenced and affected. Contact with their word opens up and extends the frontiers of our own existence and gives us a new freedom. It enables us to see things as they see them and to understand the language of things as they understand it. The true word is a source of light and life for the whole of mankind.

We know that God is not a blind life-force, but a living and personal God and, as such, he too has a Word. The essence and function of God's Word is to reveal himself to us: "No man hath seen God at any time; the only begotten Son who is in the bosom of the Father, he hath declared him." (John 1.18.) Whoever receives Jesus as the Word of God and listens to this Word is drawn into the mystery and the world of the living God. He will be born again as a child of God. (See John 1.12,13.)

This receptivity towards Jesus as the incarnate Word of God has been known, since the very beginning of the Christian era, by the name of "faith". There is no essential difference between our faith today and that of the first disciples. All faith is a gift of God's grace and a light by which we are able to perceive the invisible mystery of God's redemptive love within the visible apparition of Jesus, his death and resurrection. Before we can be aware of the tremendous breakthrough of the "power of God and the wisdom of God" in "Christ crucified, unto the Jews a stumbling-block and unto the Gentiles foolishness" (1 Cor. 1.22–4), however, we must be radically converted. This conversion can be brought about in us only by God's Spirit. Only the Spirit of God is capable of attuning our minds to God's way of thinking and acting which is so totally different from man's way: "For the foolishness of God is wiser than men; and the weakness of God is stronger than men." (1 Cor. 1.25.) The only real difference between our faith and that of the first disciples, then, is the manner in which this faith comes to us historically and psychologically. We today have not actually witnessed with our own eyes the saving event accomplished by Jesus of Nazareth and, for this reason, we receive our faith by means of the Christian message, through the preaching of the Gospel. *Fides ex auditu*—in the words of St Paul, "Faith cometh by hearing; and hearing by the word of Christ." (Rom. 10.17.) We, by our faith, and the Apostles, by their faith, are all incorporated into one great community, with and through Jesus, with the Father. St John, in the opening lines of his first epistle, emphasizes this very point: "That which was from the beginning, which we have heard, which we have seen with our own eyes, which we have looked upon and our hands have handled, of the Word of life; for the life was manifested; and we have seen and do bear witness and declare unto you the life eternal . . . That which we have seen and have heard, we declare unto you; that you also may have fellowship with us, and our fellowship may be with the Father and with his Son Jesus Christ." (1 John 1.1–3.)

This assembly gathered round the Word of God, this community, which is continuously growing as a result of the proclamation of this Word, is what we call the Church.

To summarize, then, we may truthfully say that present-day theology is characterized by a reassessment, firmly based on the Bible, of (1) the economy of grace viewed in the light of the history of salvation, (2) the concept of revelation and (3) the idea of the Word of God and that of the proclamation of the message.

This reappraisal of the three basic categories of all theological thought has also had a considerable effect on recent ecclesiological studies—some incidental evidence of this must have emerged from the foregoing, despite the brevity of the exposition. The new theology has drawn the attention of theologians to the importance of the scriptural idea of the Church and has thrown fresh light upon the whole question of the place and the function of the Church in the order of salvation.

THE CHURCH'S PLACE IN THE ORDER OF SALVATION

The entire question of the place and function of the Church in the plan of salvation, expressed in simpler terms, can be said to amount ultimately to this: What do we mean when we refer by name to the Church in the Creed, when, after confessing our faith in God the Father, God the Son and God the Holy Ghost, we directly relate the Church to

.this faith in the Trinity in the words *Credo sanctam Ecclesiam*?

This question is, of course, extremely important and the answer is by no means so easy as it might at first sight appear to be. How, we may ask, can our faith, which is a theological virtue whose object is God, also have the Church, which is the community of the faithful here on earth, as its object? Is there not an inherent danger in our equating a section of the visible and fallible human race with the invisible and transcendental mystery of God and in ascribing what may amount to a magical power to certain human actions and rites?

The answer to this question is in fact to be found in the divine economy of grace considered within the context of the history of salvation.

The essential object of our faith is, of course, God, as our saviour and salvation, who alone is able to deliver us from our mortal and sinful existence. That is why faith is a theological virtue with God as its object. It is a complete trust in and surrender to God himself, a total submission made in obedience to God's incarnate Word and in readiness to be influenced and moved by his

Spirit. For the Christian, belief is belief in God, but in a God who has shown his will to save and his saving acts to man in the course of history. In other words, men have been his visible mediators in historical situations. In the Old Testament, God was proclaimed by the men of God. With the coming of the fullness of time, he made himself known to men by the incarnation of his Word, by the mission of the Apostles with a view to the later spread of the message and by the influence of the Spirit which accompanies faith in the proclamation of the Gospel. God's saving activity depends upon man's co-operation—"God has need of men." God is not a magical power, but a mystery of word and love. Man, conversely, is not a passive thing of nature, but word and freedom. He has the capacity to listen, to approve and to pass on to others what he has heard and approved. All this is contained in the idea of "obedience in faith". By his faith, the believer is, as it were, drawn into a living dialogue with God. He opens his mind to God's Word and puts himself at the service of this Word. In Holy Scripture, the ideas of *fides* (faith), *electio* (election, vocation) and *ministerium* (service) are indissolubly united.

What may we conclude from this? We may well infer that God's saving activity, the manifestation of God's redeeming presence in the world, not only brings about a sacred history, but also calls a holy community—the Church—into being. The Church is in no way accidental in the order of salvation. It is the living community of those who, having received the Word of God, are drawn into the service of the Word. As living witnesses, they carry the message out into the world. The Church is the visible community of the faithful and, as such, is a reality in the history of salvation. It is the holy temple, "built up of living stones", the house of God on earth, the place from which God, through his Word and his Spirit, goes out to meet the world by means of the proclamation of the message. Belief in the Church means that we believe in God's redeeming presence in the Church.

It is not surprising that, whenever reference is made in Scripture to the Church, the images and concepts used are invariably derived from the history of salvation, both in form and meaning. Three phrases in particular are employed in Holy Scripture to describe the essence of the Church and to indicate her place in the whole order of salvation. These phrases refer directly to the history of salvation and tell us much more than abstract definitions could ever tell us.

In the epistles of SS Paul and Peter, the Church is generally represented as the "new People of God", that is, the group of people who have taken over the place and function of ancient Israel. This new Israel has not come about by virtue of biological descent, but has been born of baptism and faith and has come together as a "holy people". St Paul insists that the Christian believers are the true sons of Abraham and bases his claim on the following facts. In the first place, they have listened to God's Word and obeyed its summons. Secondly, they have entered into the service of this Word. Thirdly, they are ready, in the service of the Word, to proclaim the joyous message to the world and to testify to this message with their lives and their blood. The proclamation of this message is, in St Paul's view, the fulfilment of the promises made to Abraham.

A second image which is frequently used in Holy Scripture to denote the Church, is that of the "Bride of God" or the "Bride of Christ". (Eph. 5.25: 2 Cor. 11.2: Apoc. 21.2.) This expression too is derived from the Old

Testament, where it was used to indicate the unity existing between God and his chosen people. Whereas Israel was God's bride under the Old Covenant, the Church of the New Covenant is the bride of Christ. This does not, however, only mean that the Church is Christ's beloved, for whom he delivered himself up in order to sanctify her. (See Eph. 5.25.) It also implies that she is his close associate who, true to God's Word, co-operates with him in the service of this Word.

The third image is perhaps the most meaningful of all. The Church, as the new Israel of God, is the true heiress of the promise which Yahweh made to Abraham: "I will be with thee." (Exod. 3.12.) She is, from the first moment of her establishment, the "holy dwelling-place of God among men": the temple of God, the tabernacle of God among men, Jerusalem, the heavenly city. (See 1 Pet. 2.4: Apoc. 21.3.) A dwelling-place is the place where one lives and works—in other words, the place in which one shows one's presence to the world and places oneself and one's work at the service of others. The Church, as the living community of the faithful, is the holy place on earth where God, as it were, dwells in the place of men, reveals himself and communicates to men, brings about the salvation of the world by means of his Word and his Spirit and hears and answers the prayers of his children.

In all these three biblical images and concepts, the same three-dimensional reference can be discerned. Each refers back, in the first place, to the Old Covenant and to the part played by Israel in the Old Covenant. Each contains a second, direct reference to the renewal and the fulfilment of this first covenant through the incarnation of the Word of God, his death and resurrection, and the descent of the Holy Ghost. Thirdly, each refers forward to the ultimate revelation of God's kingship and glory at the end of time. All these references to the Church, then, are at the same time intrinsic references to God's saving activity throughout history. In her capacity of God's new Israel, the Church represents the second phase in the history of salvation. She can even be said to represent the permanent or "eschatological" phase, in the sense that the realities of salvation—the risen Christ, the authentic preaching of the Word and the activity of the Holy Ghost—are already present in the world, at least *in sacramento*, that is, under sacred signs and acts. In a word, the

Church, as a living community of faith, worship and love, is the sacrament of God's redeeming presence on earth. The Church, therefore, forms a part of the mystery of faith and is consequently named in the Creed: *Credo sanctam Ecclesiam*.

Clearly, an ecclesiology which stresses the historical significance of the Church within the plan of salvation must have numerous advantages and must be particularly well adapted to the times we are living in. Ecclesiologists have achieved this success by concentrating on an idea of the Church which not only incorporates, preserves and reaffirms the two abovementioned definitions (the Church as a visible, officially organized society and the Church as the mystical body of Christ), but also synthesizes these definitions at a higher level.

It is obvious, then, that ecclesiologists are far better equipped now than ever before to illuminate and to solve the traditional paradoxes and problems, and all the apparent contradictions which have vexed theologians in the past. The most difficult of these paradoxes are, of course, those concerning the visible and the invisible nature of the Church, the supernatural quality of the saving event and the hierarchical organization of the Church society, faith and sacramental life,[1] holiness and sinfulness,[2] unity and disunity. There should be no need to stress the extreme importance of these problems in the matter of ecumenical discussion.

Bearing in mind what has been said in the foregoing paragraphs, it should not be too difficult to show that these problems do not really present us with a dilemma which we have to solve by choosing either one or the other of two logically irreconcilable terms. What we are dealing with here is far more a question in the form of dialectical antithesis. In this form, we are presented with the antithesis of two mutually evocative terms which refer to and throw light upon each other. This implies that they have to be synthesized at a higher level. Antitheses of this kind are also fruitful antitheses. They set us thinking along better, purer lines and enable us to

[1] See, among others, the works of E. H. Schillebeeckx: *De sacramentele heilseconomie*, Antwerp (1952); *Christ the Sacrament*, London and New York (1963).

[2] See, for example, Karl Rahner, *Kirche der Sünder*, Freiburg im Breisgau (1948): G. Philips, *Naar een volwassen Christendom*, Davidsfonds, Louvain (1960), pp. 209ff.

approach the truth far more closely. They protect us from the danger of forming a too rigid conception of things, a conception which can so easily imprison us in an abstract conceptualism, instead of enabling us to penetrate these concepts and come closer to the reality which transcends them. This reality, which has to be approached through the abovementioned paradoxes, is no more or less than the paradox of God's invisible presence becoming visible in human history. In short, it is the mystery of God's saving activity through the mediation of the Church.

THE BUILDING UP OF THE CHURCH

The idea of *aedificatio Ecclesiae*—the building up of the Church—is not only indispensable, but also fruitful. It is indeed basic to any conception of ecclesiology.

Indeed, the whole of the foregoing argument should have established that the Church is not a dead or static reality, but a task devolving on the whole of the faithful community. This task can only be accomplished by a surrender to God's Word, in readiness to be influenced and moved by God's Spirit and in adherence to the tradition of faith

2

which can bring us back again to the original
Faith of the Apostles and the primitive Christian community.

From this, then, we have the idea of the
aedificatio Ecclesiae, as a "spiritual temple
built up of living stones". (1 Pet. 2.5.) The
work of building up the Church is never
finished. Each succeeding generation of mankind has to face the task of freely accepting
its humanity. Similarly, each generation,
loyal to the tradition which has been handed
down to it, must take over afresh the work
of building up the Church of God. For every
generation, the first priority in this task is
always the same. It is to build the Church up
into what she ought to be, so that she may
conform to God's ideas about her and so that
her essential nature may be reflected in her
outward appearance. The Church must be:

(1) The new People of God, or the new
Israel according to the Spirit. This means
that the Church must be a community of the
free children of God whose faith in Christ's
word has become the principle by which they
renew their lives both inwardly and outwardly. To express this idea in biblical
language, the People of God will be truly
reborn and resurrected, and their lives will

consequently be marked by joy, peace and concern for others.

(2) The Bride of Christ. By this we mean that the Church will love her Lord and be his partner, co-operating closely with him in his work of spreading the message of joy which can bring about God's truth and freedom in the world.

(3) God's dwelling-place among men. The Church will thus be the place on earth where something of the *mysterium tremendum et fascinosum* will visibly appear, because God is worshipped there "in spirit and truth" and, what is more, because the fruits of this worship are visible for all to see. The Church will, in short, be a holy and living temple of God, rising up in the world as a sign and an organ of God's salvation among men.

The phrase *aedificatio Ecclesiae* has, therefore, to be understood here in the broadest possible sense. It does not merely refer to the spread of the Church throughout the world by a quantitative increase in the number of believers, nor should it be taken to refer only to the social and juridical growth of the Christian community itself. An equally important aspect of the task is the qualitative building up of the community's life of faith, charity and worship, for "by the fruit the tree is known". (Matt. 12.33.) The fruits of God's Word and Spirit are "love, joy, peace, patience, benignity and goodness, mildness, faithfulness and continence", as St Paul wrote in his letter to the Galatians. (5.22.) Finally, according to the teaching of St John in his first epistle, it is first and foremost through the Christian love of one's neighbour—the constant and effective concern for one's fellow men—that the mystery of God's love will become visible on earth.

It should, then, be quite obvious that this *aedificatio Ecclesiae*, conceived in this way, must be a work embracing the whole of the Church—the entire community of Christian believers, both priests and laymen.

2

THE PRIEST

THE relationship between priests and laymen in the Church has certainly improved a great deal since the emergence of the Catholic Action movement, but one perfectly valid question has to be asked: Has the progress in mutual relations perhaps been made too much in one direction? It cannot be denied that priests, as a whole, have gradually come to understand the laity better, but there is less evidence of an increased understanding of the priest on the part of the laity. It is quite possible that the continuous emphasis which has been placed on the importance of the lay apostolate has tended to overshadow the no less important role of the priesthood and the place in the Church of religious vocations. What is more, the religious significance of freely undertaken celibacy is frequently questioned today, especially by those who are strongly influenced by contemporary psychology and the undeniable achievements of psychologists in bringing the sexual aspect of human life out of the obscurity in which it was for so long shrouded. These factors may well be responsible, to some extent at least, for the present-day shortage of vocations to the priesthood. In any case, one thing seems to me to be quite certain—the remarkable reappraisal of the role of the lay apostolate has not been accompanied by a parallel reappreciation of the office of the priesthood. And this is of the greatest importance indeed for the building up of the Church.

Although a reappraisal of the role of the clergy is vitally necessary, it must not take the form of a return to medieval Christianity or of a longing for the past. In the Middle Ages, the clergy was not only responsible for the proclamation of God's word and the administration of the sacraments. Education too was almost entirely in the hands of the clergy and a considerable part of the national wealth was controlled by priests.[1] The clergy formed an intellectual élite and was deeply involved

[1] Up to the time of the French Revolution, for example, two-thirds of France was owned by one or other of the two feudal orders, the clergy and the nobility, both of whom were exempt from the *taille*, or land-tax.

in government, administration of the State
and political life generally. This situation
persisted long after the decline of the feudal
system. Throughout the whole of the *Ancien
Régime*, the clergy was represented in the
States-General in most European countries
and formed the first "order", the highest rank
or class within society. The respect which the
clerical order enjoyed was due less to the
religious dignity of the priesthood than to
the privileged social position of the clergy.
It goes without saying that, in a secularized
and socially and politically confused world
such as ours today, the authority of the clergy
—both within the Church community and
outside it—must of necessity rest on quite
different foundations. The members of the
faithful community must acquire a clearer
understanding of the hierarchical structure
of the Church in general and of the office of
the priesthood in particular. The priest, on
the other hand, must learn to realize that his
authority rests on an authentic experience of
his vocation and mission.

THE HIERARCHY IN THE CHURCH

The ecclesiastical "hierarchy" consists of
an order of holy offices and functions which

together form a single, meaningful whole. The Hierarchy was not simply created within the Church during the course of history. It forms an essential part of the Church. At least as far as the most universal and basic features of the Hierarchy are concerned, it can be traced back to the Apostles themselves.

It is, however, impossible to understand the full significance of this ecclesiastical hierarchy so long as one confines oneself to purely juridical considerations. It is, for example, simply not sufficient to claim, as a basis for the Hierarchy, that the Church, established by Christ, is a "perfect society" and, as such, inconceivable without an organized authority. A statement of this kind gives no hint at all of the ultimate reason for the existence of the ecclesiastical hierarchy or of its basic and specific significance. An ecclesiology which depends on the idea of a perfect society not only suffers from the disadvantage of speaking a basically unscriptural language. Above all, it is trying to approach Christ's Church with concepts which are derived from secular society, and is bound to give the impression that the Church, as a hierarchically organized community, is no more than a transference onto the religious level of what is done in secular society on the purely profane level. The Church cannot be understood in this way. She is something quite different.

The Church is, as we have seen, essentially the "new People of God", the "Israel according to the Spirit", the "living temple of God in the midst of men". There is a place in this Church for a "hierarchy", or an organized entity of sacred offices and functions. The very essence of the new Israel gave rise to this organization. Even more particularly, the "hierarchy" was the direct result of the way in which the new People of God came into being and of the saving function which this people was called upon to fulfil in the world. The new Israel of God did not, after all, grow and prosper because of any biological descent, but by preaching and proclaiming the word of God in which it believed. In the words of St Paul, "Faith cometh by hearing; and hearing by the word of Christ." (Rom. 10.17.) This preaching, under Christ's orders, was entrusted by Christ himself to his apostles until the end of time. This was indeed the last message which Jesus bequeathed to the Eleven, his spiritual testament: "All power is given to me in heaven and on earth. Going, therefore, teach ye all nations; baptizing them

in the name of the Father and of the Son and
of the Holy Ghost; teaching them to observe
all things whatsoever I have commanded you.
And behold, I am with you all days, even to
the consummation of the world." (Matt.
28.18–20.) St John expresses this even more
tersely: "As the Father hath sent me, I also
send you" (John 20.21), adding, for St Peter,
"Feed my sheep". (21.17.) St Paul rightly
regarded himself as an apostle equal to "the
Twelve", because he too was "called" by
Christ to be an apostle and to proclaim the
"gospel of God". (Rom. 1.1.) The vocation
and the mission of the Apostles were in no
sense an accidental circumstance in the divine
plan of salvation, but an essential part of it.
According to St Paul, it was God "who hath
reconciled us to himself by Christ and hath
given to us [the Apostles] the ministry of reconciliation", and the commission to preach
reconciliation, making us Christ's ambassadors. God exhorts others by the word of the
Apostles to be reconciled to him and, co-
operating with God as his partners, the
Apostles "exhort you that you receive not the
grace of God in vain". (2 Cor. 5.18:6.1.)

In a word, the Church of Christ is founded
on her "apostolic mission" or "embassy". It

is a mission which began with the mission of Jesus, who was sent by the Father. Through the Apostles and their successors, this mission is still carried out in the various ramifications of the many offices and functions of the Hierarchy.[1] The Church, says St Paul, is "built upon the foundation of the Apostles and Prophets, Jesus Christ himself being the chief corner-stone". (Eph. 2.20.) The Church, then, is inseparable from the Apostles and their successors. These men, who have been appointed by the Apostles with the help of the divine Spirit, are similarly entrusted with the task of preaching the Gospel even to the consummation of the world. They too are responsible for keeping the Faith pure and whole, for the continued celebration of the Lord's Supper and for the maintenance of order within the Church. In all this they are guided by the Holy Spirit.

What conclusions may we draw from this? First and foremost that the presence of a hierarchy within the Church is completely different from the presence of any governmental authority in secular society, both in origin

[1] The word "apostle" comes, of course, from the Greek *apostolos*, meaning an ambassador, one who is sent.

and in significance. All secular governments
derive their authority in the long run from
the people. The political society is created
by human civilization—it is the home which
humanity builds for itself. The people are
there first. They create the Government for
themselves and invest it with authority and
power. In the case of the Church, the process
is reversed. As the home of God among men,
the Church is not a creation of human civilization, but the work of God's Word and
Spirit. Divinely created, she continues to
exist by "hearing by the word of Christ".
The people, in other words, were not there
first, but the preaching of the message under
Christ's orders, that is to say, the preaching of
his ambassadors and those who are specially
invested with the office of co-operating with
him. It is as a result of this preaching that
the people, gathered round this preaching,
grow into a holy and priestly people. To
quote St Paul once again: "In Christ Jesus,
by the Gospel, I have begotten you." (1 Cor.
4.15.)

We may then conclude that there is no
essential conflict between the so-called "universal priesthood" of the Church as a holy
community and the presence within this com-

munity of a hierarchy, or order of holy offices
and functions.[1]

THE OFFICE OF THE PRIESTHOOD

The question which we must now consider
is this: What is the real significance of the
priestly office within the Hierarchy? We shall
limit our discussion primarily to the vocation
and function of the diocesan priesthood,
which, in the Western Church, has developed
a definite shape and form and a certain meaningful religious unity. It is with this idea of
meaningful religious unity in mind that we
shall examine the subject.

For many people, the priest is someone
who, by virtue of his ordination, has received the power to celebrate Mass and, on
condition that he has been given the necessary
faculty, to hear confessions. That he is com-
missioned to carry out any other apostolic
task over and above this is, in the common
view, purely accidental; many see it as a kind
of extra duty performed in the employment
of the Church. As far as the celibacy of the
priesthood is concerned, a very large number

[1] See E. J. de Smedt, *Het priesterschap van de
gelovigen*, Tielt and Lannoo (1961).

of people believe that this is no more than an obligation imposed upon the priest by the Western Church, similar to the rules of fasting and abstinence. Such a view of the priesthood is both superficial and unfair, because it isolates the various components of the priestly office which in fact form a single, meaningful whole. This unity of meaning is of the greatest importance, since it is this which gives each of the individual components its own significance.

Seen, then, as a meaningful religious unity, the priestly vocation is, at the deepest level, an apostolic and ecclesiastical vocation. It is essentially a total gift, based on a divine vocation, of one's whole life to God and the Church for the sake of God's work of salvation. Three elements of this definition merit closer consideration: (1) The universal idea of life-vocation. (2) The idea of an apostolic and ecclesiastical vocation. (3) The idea of a total gift to God and the Church in response to the divine call.

(1) The idea of vocation. The priestly office, like every function within the divine economy of salvation, can always be traced back to a divine vocation, or an initiative on God's part through grace. *Nemo vocatur nisi*

a Deo: "Neither doth any man take the honour
to himself, but he that is called by God, as
Aaron was." (Heb. 5.4.) St Paul's reference
to the priesthood of the Old Testament is extremely significant. The God of Abraham,
Isaac and Jacob was not a magical power, but
a living and personal God, a mystery of Word
and Spirit. God's saving activity, therefore,
is not a succession of magical occurrences, but
a divine intervention in the history of man
through the medium of living men informed
and motivated by the grace of God. It is thus
possible to see, in the Old Testament, how
the two concepts, *ministerium* (office, function) and *electio* (election or vocation), always
go together and how both point to the important place of and the leading part played by
the men of God in Israel.

Now, Christianity has never abandoned
this extremely important idea of vocation in-
herited from the Old Testament, and the
Church has continuously combated the ever-
recurring danger that her offices may become
over-technical and too functionalized. This
is powerfully illustrated, for example, by the
great care which the post-Tridentine Church
has always shown in the training of her
priests. This deep concern is reflected not

only in the importance attached to the education of future priests in theology and in personal holiness, but also in the even greater emphasis which the Church places on making absolutely sure that her candidates for the priesthood have—to use the popular phrase —a "real vocation". In other words, only the purest and most authentic religious motives are accepted as valid in the case of vocations to the priesthood.

It is most helpful to bear in mind, in our attempt to reach a better understanding of the profound significance of the idea of "vocation", that the concept is not confined exclusively to the purely religious sphere of human activity. *Mutatis mutandis,* the idea of "vocation" is to be found everywhere in the world, wherever men strive to escape from the banal, anonymous existence of a too technical society and try to achieve a more personal and authentic pattern of life. Vocation is the origin and the guarantee of a genuine life. We have only to think of the poet whose writing is no longer the outcome of a poet's vocation, but has become no more than clever versification, of the philosopher whose work no longer consists of a personal struggle with truth, but has sunk to the level of mere scholastic exercise, of the doctor who has lost sight of his vocation to heal and uses his profession simply as a means of making money. All great human enterprises are the result of vocation. Vocation is an inner call. It is an inward voice, speaking to man, moving him and inspiring him, making him, as it were, place himself at the service of the universe. When it is motivated by a sense of vocation, human activity manifests itself outwardly as a personal task, a mission and a service. "I have a work to do" was how Newman expressed it. For Heidegger, man, as a *weltbildend* being, was not primarily *Entwurf*— design, plan, enterprise, creative initiative— but *Sorge,* concern for a particular value and capacity to heed the call of that value. According to Gabriel Marcel, the creativity of the artist is a question of fidelity. It is above all this fidelity which can prevent a man from falling a victim to the anonymity of an over-technical bureaucratic society and can positively enable him to conceive his particular office or function as a personal vocation, and thus to impress the stamp of his own personality upon it. A sense of vocation is therefore more than a point of departure for a personal choice of a certain way of life. It is also the enduring source of inspiration throughout the whole of the individual's life of the spirit. In this sense, a conscious vocation has a social significance and contributes towards the formation of the community. Expressed more simply, the true poet, artist, philosopher or social worker, conscious of his life and work as vocation, is "grace" for the people with whom he comes in contact. The springs which feed the life of the spirit run dry whenever man ceases to be aware of his vocation.

All this applies to an even greater extent to religious life. The priest who is no longer open to the *mysterium tremendum et fascinosum*, who loses his sense of the living God, always becomes a prey to empty ritualism and formalism. Many people nowadays lament the fact that there are so few vocations to the religious life and the priesthood. But the situation would be far worse if men were to lose their sense of religious vocation. It is possible to say that the most important task of the priestly vocation is to check the tendency in the religious life of the Christian community to become too technical and too functionalized and to keep alive that communal sense of vocation without which genuine

Christianity is impossible. Christianity—
and this applies, too, to lay Christianity—is
the result of divine grace, and divine grace is
God's call to us, a call which we hear and to
which we, in faith, give our positive answer.
The vocation of the priest is, at the deepest
level, the call of God's grace to a true and
authentic life of faith, a living with and for
God in subjection to God's Word and in
openness to the influence of God's Spirit.
This is what is meant by *oboedientia fidei*.
To summarize, then, the first duty of the
priest, as a leader of the flock, is to keep alive
in the minds of the members of his flock that
vital sense of God, to nourish this consciousness of God and to appear in the world as a
man of God. It need hardly be added that all
that we have said here on the subject of religious vocation applies not only to priests
but to all men and women in religious com-
munities.[1]

(2) The priest's vocation is also a directly
apostolic and ecclesiastical vocation. This
means that the primary aim of this vocation

[1] It applies most particularly, too, to the so-called
contemplative vocations. Their especial task is to
preserve the evangelical consciousness of God in all
its purity and perfection.

is not the personal perfection of the recipient of the vocation, but the spread of the Christian message and the *cura animarum*, or pastoral care of the Christian flock. The priestly vocation, then, is first and foremost directed towards the *aedificatio Ecclesiae*, the building up of the Church into a genuine community of faith, worship and apostolic activity.

The term "apostolic vocation" should be understood in this context in its original significance, that is to say, as an extension of the great classical missionary texts of the Old and New Testaments. Jesus did not call his apostles and send them out on their mission in order that they should settle in the desert and work for the salvation of their own souls. He called them to enter into the service of the Kingdom of God: "Come ye after me, and I will make you to be fishers of men" (Matt. 4.19): "All power is given to me . . . Going, therefore, teach ye all nations, baptizing them . . . Behold, I am with you all days." (Matt. 28.18–20.) "You have not chosen me; but I have chosen you", were the words of Jesus according to the Gospel of St John, "and I have appointed you, that you should go and should bring forth fruit; and your fruit should remain." (John 15.16.) The apostle, once he has been called, no longer belongs to himself. He is always at God's disposal and must serve God in the work of his salvation. To quote the words which Cardinal Mercier addressed to his priests: "The priest achieves his own salvation in bringing about the salvation of others."[1]

This apostolic vocation of the priest is at the same time a directly ecclesiastical vocation—a vocation which is immediately concerned with the Church. "The Pope and the bishops are the external organs of the divine vocation."[2] This observation by Cardinal Mercier strikes at the heart of the matter. The Church, and the building up of the Church, are the object of every vocation which has been sanctioned and confirmed by the Church. "Whenever a bishop accepts a candidate for the priesthood and ordains him, he bestows upon him a mission whose origin is divine", a mission in the tradition of that "entrusted

---

[1] Cardinal Mercier, *La Vie intérieure, Appel aux âmes sacerdotales*, Brussels (1919), pt. 1, p. 184: "La forme spéciale de notre charité apostolique peut se traduire en cette devise: nous sauver en sauvant les autres."

[2] Mercier, p. 188.

by Christ to the Apostles and their successors".[1]

It is, of course, possible to distinguish between the various functions within this mission—the preaching of the Gospel, the administration of the sacraments, the maintenance of order within the Christian community and so on. All these functions, however, form together a single meaningful unity. The traditional concepts of *cura animarum*, pastoral office or pastoral care, express this basic unity of all the missionary functions of the priest.

There is, of course, an implicit reference in this idea of "pastoral office" to the vocation and mission of Jesus himself, the shepherd of the new People of God. "I am the good shepherd . . . Therefore doth the Father love me; because I lay down my life [for my sheep], that I may take it again." (John 10.14,17.) What emerges quite clearly from this image of the "good shepherd" is that Jesus's position of authority within the economy of salvation cannot be adequately expressed in terms of power and law. What it does is to lead us into the mystery of God's providence and love: "The good shepherd giveth his life for his sheep . . . I am the good

[1] Mercier, p. 188.

shepherd; and I know mine, and mine know me, as the Father knoweth me, and I know the Father." (John 10.11,14,15.) The same is bound to apply to those to whom the care of the Lord's flock has been committed now, in the name of the Lord. These are, first and foremost, the bishops, to whom a part of this flock has been entrusted. This is why the function of the episcopate cannot be fully defined in terms which are derived exclusively from legal language. The bishop is taken up in a lasting and permanent manner, by his election, consecration by anointing and canonical appointment, into the mysterious love-relationship which binds Christ on the one hand to his Father and on the other hand to his Church, his Father's flock. This is why the bishop is called the "shepherd", or "pastor", and the "bridegroom", of his church. In this capacity, he solemnly pledges himself to care for the spiritual life of his flock and, following the example of the Lord, to be ready to lay down his life for that flock. According to St Thomas, this is the essence of the pastoral office: "It belongs to the pastoral office that one should lay down his life for his flock."[1]

[1] *Summa Theol.*, 2a, 2ae, q. 184, a. 5.

It is, of course, perfectly obvious that no bishop is able to exercise this pastoral function—which, though forming a single, meaningful unity, includes the spread of the Faith by preaching, the administration of the sacraments and the wise government of the Christian community in his diocese—entirely alone and unaided. He is helped in this task by his priests. In ordaining these men and appointing them to their office, he entrusts them with a part or aspect of his pastoral function. To quote again from what Cardinal Mercier had to say to his priests: "As your bishop's collaborators, you are consciously and intimately associated with his apostolate and, like him, animated by the same love of the Church. This love should spur you on to offer up your life for your flock."[1] It is this part of the priest's function which we must now consider.

(3)   The priest's total gift of his life. The priest's function is firmly based on divine vocation. It is God who, by means of his grace, takes the initiative and calls the man to become a priest. This does not mean, however, that the man is denied the freedom to respond to this call. As we have already

[1] Mercier, p. 204.

observed, God is not a magic power, but a mystery of Word and Love. When God turns towards man and addresses his Word to him, he does not destroy his freedom. On the contrary, he releases him so that he may carry out the work of divine salvation. In this way, a new dimension is added to human freedom. The man who responds to God's call is given a new and wider scope. This encounter between God's Word and man's positive consent, this creation of a new dimension, is what is known, in theology, as *oboedientia fidei*, the virtue of faith. All apostolic service is accomplished in faith. When we say that the priest must appear in the world as a man of God, we mean that he must be a man of faith and prayer. Faith is not simply a question of knowledge. Going beyond knowledge, it is an attitude of receptivity, readiness and alert watchfulness with regard to God's Word and Spirit. It is, then, an attitude of trusting surrender to God. The man of faith allows God, as it were, to be in his life.

The apostolic vocation, in the biblical sense of the phrase, is distinguished by the fact that it claims the *whole* man. This implies that the person who is called is bound to give his unreserved consent and to surrender his life totally and unconditionally to God and to God's work of salvation. According to St Luke, the Apostles left all things in order to follow Christ. (See Luke 5.11.) St Paul was, as it were, removed from the secular world and unconditionally set aside— ". . . separated unto the Gospel of God". (Rom. 1.1.)

As for Christ himself, his entire life was an unhesitating surrender to the saving will of his Father: "I come to do thy will, O God." (Heb. 10.5–9.) This was the sole *Leitmotiv* of his whole life from the moment that he came into the world (see Heb. 10.5) until the moment that, exhausted and abandoned, he gave up his spirit on the Cross ("being made obedient unto death").

Following the example of the "Behold, I come" of his Lord and in union with it, the priest gives his consent to God when he is called to his ordination by his bishop. This consent implies a total gift of himself to God, the total commitment of his entire being to the service of God's saving work.

The voluntary celibacy to which the priest pledges himself at this time is the symbol and the instrument of his total gift of himself to God and the divine work of salvation. The

sole aim of this voluntarily undertaken, permanent celibacy is to give a lasting form and
an extended meaning and full scope to the
totality of this gift of self to God. The celibacy
of the priesthood has a positive meaning in
this context. It should never, in any sense, be
interpreted as a condemnation or a belittle-
ment of the married state. The priest's voluntary renunciation of marriage for the sake of
the Kingdom of God (see Matt. 19.12) has a
deep and positive implication. Not only does
he place all his external work at the service
of God's Word. At the deeper level too, he
keeps himself free and reserves his most profound emotive powers and his capacity to love
for the love of God and of all his neighbours.
He places himself, as a celibate, at the universal service of the whole of mankind. The fact
that he pledges himself to this in the form of
a religious vow means too that this total gift
of himself, although it embraces his entire
life as a priest from its very beginning *usque
ad mortem*, is at the same time a task, a commission which has to be accomplished in
time and must therefore be taken up every
day anew in good faith.

This has, however, all to be done for the
sake of the message—". . . separated unto the

Gospel of God". (Rom. 1.1.) The fact that the priest is, as it were, "set aside" and, as a consequence of his celibate state, has to live a "separate" life, should never lead him to "separation" from his fellow men. His closeness to God must, according to the whole of Christian teaching, bring him closer to men: "As long as you did it to one of these my least brethren, you did it to me." (Matt. 25.40.) These are Christ's own words. The words of the ancient Latin poet, too, apply particularly to the priest: *Homo sum, humani nihil a me alienum puto*—"I am a man, and nothing that is human is foreign to me." It will be, of course, at once obvious that celibacy may stand in the way of a closer relationship with other men. In its positive aspect, however, it can lead the priest towards a greater openness of mind and indeed towards a deeper wisdom in his relationship with others and can help him to become more intimate with them. One of the dangers which constantly threatens the priest is, as we have already pointed out, that of a routine, technical approach to his office. In addition to this, the priest is always exposed to the danger of becoming complacent and pedantic in his attitude towards others. That is why study and honest, open

dialogue with the laity and those who are not
of his faith are so important for the priest. By
study I do not mean scholarship so much as
an attitude of alert openness to the truth,
wherever this truth may come from, spring-
ing from a genuine love of truth. (The basic
meaning of the Latin word *studere* is, after
all, "to apply oneself with interest to".) To
quote yet again the words of that great man,
Cardinal Mercier is recorded to have said,
two years before his death, on the occasion of
the fiftieth anniversary of his ordination as
a priest: "These are the sources from which
I have drawn everything of any use that I
have ever been able to say or do in my life—
a love of the truth, pure, straightforward
truth without fear or bravado, and a love of
those souls given to me to love by the Good
Shepherd himself."[1] On his own testimony,
then, we may know that these two loves—a
love for souls and a love of truth—were the
two springs which fed the priestly life of this
great Prince of the Church and enabled it to

[1] "Voici les sources auxquelles j'ai puisé tout ce
que j'ai pu dire ou réaliser d'utile dans ma vie:
l'amour de la vérité, de la vérité toute pure, sans
ambages, sans peur ni bravade; l'amour des âmes
que le Pasteur suprême m'avait données à aimer."

bear such abundant fruit. Only those things which had their source in these two living springs seemed to him to have any value: "Everything of any use that I have ever been able to say or do in my life, I have drawn from these sources." Springs are the secret places on earth where life has its source. If the springs dry up, life dies and everything becomes barren and soulless. This applies not only to nature, but also to civilization and to the religious life. Without love and study, the priest becomes a soulless official. However much he may talk, he will have nothing to say. However much he may do, he will achieve nothing. He will have no contact with his people.

The priest must, as we have already said, appear in the world as a man of God. We may add, he must appear as a good man, full of understanding for others.

3

THE LAYMAN IN THE CHURCH

So much has already been written in recent years about the place and function of the layman in the Church that it is very difficult indeed to find anything to say on this subject that has not been said a hundred times before.[1] It is, however, not my intention to cover the subject completely. I propose, on the contrary, to limit myself to a few important points concerning the role of the laity in theological thought, in the

[1] See, among other works, the pastoral letter of the bishops of the Netherlands on the Council, Christmas Eve, 1960; E. J. de Smedt, *Het priesterschap van de gelovigen*, Tielt and Lannoo (1961); Y. Congar, O.P., *Lay People in the Church: A Study for a Theology of Laity*, London, Bloomsbury Publishing Co. (1957); G. Philips, *De leek in de Kerk*, Louvain (1952); *Naar een volwassen Christendom*, Louvain (1960); "De leek in de moderne wereldcrisis", from the proceedings of the National Congress of the Lay Apostolate, Louvain (December, 1956); *"De leek in de Kerk. Ontwikkeling en Bewustwording doorheen de Kerkgeschiedenis"*, *Universitas-tijdschrift*, Louvain (January, 1957).

sacramental and liturgical life of the Church and in the present-day apostolate. Before I do this, however, I should like to make one or two observations on the enormous significance of the layman's "coming of age".

THE AWAKENING OF THE CHURCH IN HER LAITY

From time to time, one hears it said that the Catholic Action movement, in which the Church placed all her hope between the two wars, did not produce the results that had been expected of it. Many even go so far as to claim that the movement failed entirely. Catholic Action did not, however, fail. Its achievements were, in fact, quite considerable, but they were different from the hoped-for results. In the first place, the movement actively furthered the coming of age of the laity. In the second place, it brought about a thorough renewal and rejuvenation in the whole life of the Church. To summarize the effects of Catholic Action, the Church herself was "awakened in her laity".[1] It is quite

[1] This phrase, taken from an article by Dr Jan Grootaers, expresses very well the far-reaching change and renewal in the Church which Catholic

wrong to use the word "failure" in this connection, just as wrong as it would be to call the fact that a child does not remain a child a failure.

It is, however, especially important to note that this growth towards maturity on the part of the laity has followed two directions, each direction corresponding to one of the two basic meanings which the word "lay" has acquired in the course of history.

It is, of course, generally known that the term "lay" comes from the Greek word *laikos*. *Laikos* is derived from *laos*, which meant "people" and was used in the Greek translation of the Bible as the technical term for Israel as the People of God, in contrast to the other peoples, the so-called pagans, heathens or "Gentiles", who were characterized by the word *ethne*. Originally, then, the term "lay" did not apply to the secular world of the laity (in the modern sense). It referred to the normal members of the holy People of God.[1]

Action has brought about. (See Dr Jan Grootaers, "De Kerk ontwaakt in de leek", *Universitas-tijdschrift*, Louvain (January, 1958).)

[1] For a more precise definition, see I. de la Potterie, "L'Origine et le sens primitif du mot 'Laïc', in *Nouv. Rev. théologique* (1958), pp. 840–53.

It is, however, not so surprising that the word "lay" has eventually come to indicate the secular world, as distinct from the religious or clerical world. The monopolization of all religious offices and functions by the clergy was bound to lead to a sharp distinction between the religious order or class and the people, in the sense of the great number of ordinary believers. This antithesis between clergy and laity later hardened into a firm division between the two social orders. In certain circles, especially, for example, in post-revolutionary France, the adjective "lay" (*laïc*) became synonymous with "neutral" in the matter of faith and even "hostile" to religion, or "anti-clerical". That is why, in France today, a distinction is generally made between *laïcisme* and *laïcité*. The word *laïcisme* is used to refer to the lay attitude of hostility towards the Church, the anti-clerical attitude which seeks to divorce lay activity completely from the influence of religion. *Laïcité*, on the other hand, is the term used to indicate that attitude which recognizes the true content and legality of the secular, lay world, as distinct from the clerical world.

There is, then, a great movement afoot in the lay sphere of the Catholic Church today

towards a fully mature status. In this movement, however, it is possible to detect not
only a striving towards full adulthood within
the religious life of the Church, but also an
equally pronounced tendency to reject any
kind of inferiority in the purely secular
sphere. The Catholic layman is no longer
content to appear, in the secularized lay world
in which he lives, as a second-rate citizen. He
is struggling to combat the impression that,
because he is a Catholic, he is consequently
less independent and less capable of creative
activity than other men in the world of
science, art, literature, economics or politics.
He is vitally concerned to prove that he is as
well equipped as other men to tackle the great
problems of our day and age. It should be
noted, in this context, that, in pressing for
full adult autonomy in every sphere of secular life, the present-day layman is in no way
conceding anything to anti-clericalism in any
shape or form. On the contrary, he sees his
activity as a duty performed for his Church.
Nothing seems to him to be more dangerous
for and debasing to the Christian message
than the inertia and indifference of so many
Catholics for whom faithfulness to the Christian tradition is synonymous with a complete

lack of understanding and a narrow-minded conservatism.

In the diary of the French novelist and philosopher, Simone de Beauvoir, *Memoirs of a Dutiful Daughter,* we come across the following objection which, despite the audacity with which it is expressed, deserves to be taken very seriously. If we are to believe what this writer says concerning her apostasy from the Church, her first difficulties were due to the narrow-minded attitude which characterized the Catholic high school at which she was a pupil. As in the case of so many such institutions, a slavish submission to the school rules and discipline was apparently regarded as the highest criterion of faith and good morals. Like many other religious-minded girls of her age, Simone habitually confessed every fortnight. One day she heard her confessor, whom she had hitherto regarded as a sensible man, whisper to her: "It has come to my ears that my little Simone has changed ... that she is disobedient, noisy, that she answers back when she is reprimanded." At once Simone lost all confidence in her confessor. It was at this moment, too, that the idea which was to stay with her all her life came to her for the first time, that God was perhaps petty-minded and fussy, like a pious old woman, that he might even be stupid.[1] Nothing is more painful for the modern Catholic layman than the feeling that his image of God might perhaps be the image of a petty and narrow-minded God.

The layman's coming of age has caused a new situation to come about within the entire Church and has posed an entirely new set of problems. Catholic Action has produced an alert, bold and demanding laity, a laity which sometimes causes those who lead the community a good deal of embarrassment. Sleeping infants and well-behaved little children do not give much trouble, but it is often extremely difficult to lead a large group of mature adults. This does not, however, mean to say that the Church is better served by sleeping children!

In brief, then, the present-day layman, and particularly the intellectual layman, makes much higher demands in the religious sphere than in the past. His needs for theological understanding are frequently greater than what can be supplied in normal sermons.

[1] Simone de Beauvoir, *Memoirs of a Dutiful Daughter*, London, André Deutsch Ltd. and Weidenfeld and Nicolson Ltd. (1959), p. 136.

Anxious for purity in religion, he is quick to criticize half-hearted measures and conformist attitudes. He is impatient for liturgical reform. He wishes to see some of the historical splendour of the Liturgy, which he so much admires in the cathedrals and abbeys that he visits, introduced into his own parish church, though in new forms, freely adapted to parish life. He is dissatisfied with the piecemeal activities of his parish in this respect. No longer does he dream of a revival of the spirit of the Middle Ages—he is much more at home in the diversity of the modern world. An example of this extreme modernity of outlook is the layman's spontaneous reaction against any kind of medieval interpretation of the kingship of Christ or of the Pauline doctrine of "restoring all things in Christ". (Eph. 1.10.)

The modern Catholic layman is extremely outspoken. This attitude, stemming from the fact that he feels compelled, as an adult, to express his demands, is often interpreted wrongly as rebelliousness or anti-clericalism. A much fairer assessment of this outspokenness on the part of the modern layman would be to recognize in it his deep concern for the

Church. The Dutch bishops showed that they understood the layman's attitude in the pastoral letter of December 1960, published before the opening of the Second Vatican Council: "Your zeal to ensure that the Church should possess that radiant beauty which will enable her, in the words of Pope John XXIII, to be a gentle invitation to others, makes it possible for us also to understand the outspokenness with which the faithful criticize many of the Church's shortcomings. That there is a place in the Church for public opinion has already been explicitly conceded by Pope Pius XII.[1] We cannot, nor would we wish to, deprive you of this right . . . But your criticism should be legitimate . . . free of bitterness or rancour . . . The Catholic's criticism is an expression of his genuine love for the Church. It should never be presumptuous, but should always reflect a concern for the

[1] *Osservatore Romano*, 18 February, 1950. The statement made by Pope Pius XII, which is alluded to here, comes from an address to representatives of the Press. Among other things, the Pope said: "The Church is a living body, and something essential would be lacking in her life if there were no opportunity for the free expression of the Church's public opinion. Both the Hierarchy and the faithful would be to blame for any such shortcoming."

Church and indeed be accompanied by a certain Christian sorrow."[1]

I should like to add two comments, while on the subject of this right to criticism within the Church. Firstly, it is of the utmost importance that lay criticism and free opinion within the Church should never degenerate into a kind of "parade of the discontented". The Good News can never be disseminated by discontented bearers. Such people run the risk of making not only themselves, but also the cause they are serving, ridiculous. Secondly, it would be wrong to designate the task of the layman within the Church as that of a critic. The Christian community of faith is not a parliament in which the laity performs the function of an opposition party. This might indeed be simply another way of keeping the layman in an inferior position. In order to free him from any such position of inferiority, it would be quite wrong to impose a rule of silence upon him. There is only one possible solution, and that is to include the layman in honest and genuine dialogue. We must now consider this question more closely.

[1] *Tijdschrift voor Theologie* (January, 1961), p. 89.

THE LAYMAN IN THEOLOGICAL THOUGHT

There is certainly no need for us to prove our point when we claim that the layman is able to become a perfectly competent and mature theologian. Theology is not charismatically restricted to the priesthood. Two things are above all necessary for the formation of a good theologian. The first is a universal sensitivity, a delicacy of response towards the world of religious faith. The second is a thorough grounding in theology. It is common to find both of these in the layman. But there is more to it than this. It is not even necessary for the lay theologian to have studied every theological treatise in great detail for him to be well versed in one or other department of Christian thought. It is, moreover, by no means rare nowadays to find doctors, lawyers, scientists, scholars in the humanities and many others who have studied numerous theological works, such as the writings of Guardini, Newman, Karl Rahner, De Lubac, Daniélou and Yves Congar. It is consequently not surprising that these laymen know considerably more about certain theological questions than many priests. It should also not be regarded as a

sign of rebelliousness that such well-informed
laymen should hold different opinions from
their pastors on certain matters. I have frequently been struck by the remarkably deli-
cate and original insight which many self-
made lay theologians often have into certain
religious problems, even though such people
sometimes lack the necessary theological background to the question. It is for this reason
that dialogue between the professional theologian and people of this kind can often be so
immensely rewarding and informative.

This, of course, brings us to the heart of
the matter under discussion. It would undoubtedly be an enormous gain to the Church
if there were, in every country throughout
the world, a number of her laymen trained
in this way, men who had studied theology
at a high level. Yet this does not seem to me
to be the most important aspect of the question. It is, in my opinion, of even greater
importance today that theology should be the
outcome of a dialogue between priest and layman.

It should, however, not be forgotten in this
connection that theology has always to
some extent been the fruit of such discussion. Theology is, after all, no more than a

rationally and even scientifically developed dialogue between faith and natural reason,[1] and reason is something which all men possess. It is common to priests and to laymen, to believers and to non-believers. The message of the Faith needs dialogue. This is implied in the idea of *oboedientia fidei*. The fact that God's word is directed towards man presupposes that this word is capable of appealing to man and that man, hearing it, is able both to receive it and to give his consent to it, with the aim of assimilating it into his life. This process is, after all, a kind of dialogue between believing man and man as a rational being. To develop this idea further, faith, because it gives the most sublime and the ultimate meaning to our human existence, has the task of illuminating, inspiring and giving direction to this existence. Believing can never mean the repetition by rote of the pronouncements of Christ or the Church. It is always an intelligent understanding of these statements, an attempt to create a Christian way of thinking and living, a penetration of civilization and society by the Christian spirit

[1] In the case of St Thomas, this took the form of a dialogue between faith and Aristotelian philosophy and the medieval view of the world.

and a striving towards an ideal of Christian humanism. It implies, in other words, that the believer will behave as a Christian in relation to his fellows. This presupposes that the believer, as a free, intelligent and independent being, is constantly engaged in dialogue with faith and is constantly examining his faith, in order to reach a firmly based, consistent understanding of this faith (*fides quaerens intellectum*), an understanding of the validity of the Faith (justification of the Faith), an understanding of the truths of the Faith, its mystery and the formulation of this mystery (dogmatic theology), and finally an understanding of the demands of the Faith, insofar as the Faith ought to inspire and regulate his day-to-day actions (moral theology or Christian ethics).

This theological examination of the Faith can be made with expert scientific knowledge, in which case it is, of course, theology in the strictly scientific sense. But, in this case, it must be true to say that theology is a rationally developed science, since, as soon as faith awakens to the need to achieve a full maturity, it at once begins to consider and examine, to enlarge its horizons in Christian thought and to engage in dialogue with reason. That is why the First Vatican Council's definition of faith as an *obsequium rationale*, an intelligent, free and liberating recognition of God's Word, is strictly accurate.[1]

If, then, a true theological synthesis is only possible on this basis of dialogue between faith and natural reason, this must apply even more to our present age. We are in urgent

---

[1] It should, of course, be clear that the word "reason" is not used here in the Cartesian sense, that is to say, in the sense in which this word is employed in the rational philosophical system of Descartes and in the exact sciences which are concerned with precise and unequivocal concepts. Reason can also be understood in its broader, existential sense. In this perspective, reason can be seen as the universal openness or faculty within us which is capable of recognizing what is good and true in all its many forms, of accounting for this truth and goodness and of assimilating it freely into our human behaviour. Viewed in its existential perspective, reason can be regarded as the root of all intellectual freedom and of our power of understanding and faculty of perception. In this sense, reason is what makes us man as a rational being and what permits us to emerge from the half-sleep of anonymous existence into full personality. It is in this sense, then, that I use the word "reason", whenever I say that theology is the outcome of a dialogue between faith and reason.

need today of a renewed and rejuvenated *Summa Theologica*, a synthesis of Christian thought which, as Cardinal Suhard has said, will be a *Summa* capable of leading to intelligible dialogue with the world of today—a dialogue which will be understood by this world because it is geared to the contemporary vision of the world. I am not thinking only of the natural, purely scientific cosmology, but also of the psychological and anthropological view of our present society and above all of the feeling for ethical values which lies at the root of our present view of history. And what does this imply, if not that theology is above all the outcome of an open and honest dialogue between the priest-theologian and the lay world of today? This dialogue is absolutely indispensable in those cases—so frequently encountered and so vitally important—where faith and life come into direct contact with each other, as, for example, in problems of social justice and marriage.

I have said that this necessary dialogue should be "open and honest". By this I mean that it should be dialogue in which the layman's difficulties, objections and opinions are taken quite seriously, as elements which can make a positive contribution towards the finding of solutions. Such solutions can almost always be found, but not without careful preparation on both sides. What the layman, and especially the intellectual layman, finds so frustrating is that his part in the dialogue is often reduced to that of a pupil in a class— he is allowed to ask questions, but only in order to obtain a clear answer. Our educational system has, after all, still not reached the point where the pupil is treated as an intelligent partner in equal dialogue. As a result, it rarely happens that his difficulties are taken so seriously that an immediate answer is quite impossible and that the answer which is given is used to provide a point of departure from which the entire group seeks a solution together. But whatever the disadvantages in the traditional method of instruction may be, one thing is abundantly clear. The conscientious layman, with several years of university and practical experience in the world behind him, is no longer a child, and it is extremely likely that he will have acquired, in the lay world, a moral sensitivity and a theological insight of which few theologians in holy orders can boast.

The Layman in the Church's Sacramental and Liturgical Life

There have been many changes for the better in this sphere during the last few years, changes which augur well for the future. The most striking, of course, is the increasing share which the layman is taking in the Church's sacramental and liturgical life. Perhaps even more promising, however, is the emergence of a new doctrine of the sacraments which is developing along parallel lines to the new ecclesiology outlined in the first chapter of this book.

The Church has always regarded the "sacraments" as a number of sacred signs which not only signify the realities of salvation in the sense of representing these realities symbolically (as, for example, the "sacramental" of the crucifix symbolizes the death of Christ), but also, so to speak, contain these realities and make them present and actual for us. The words of consecration, "This is my body", do not merely remind us of what Christ did on the eve of his passion. They cause Christ to become effectively present in our midst. Hence St Augustine's definition of the sacrament as the "visible form of an invisible grace".

The fact remains, however, that man is always disposed to interpret the saving activity of the sacraments in a rather mechanical, indeed almost magical, manner and to conceive the sacraments as material things which become suddenly charged with a supernatural energy. As a result, he tends to think that a supernatural effect is brought about automatically, that is, without any free, conscious act of faith playing any part.

The emergent sacramental doctrine, to which I have already referred, is a positive reaction against this too materialistic view. Even the Catechism tells us that "sacraments are sacred acts and words". This means that they are acts of faith, used in public worship and possessing a particular sanctifying efficacy. They are acts made in the Church, in the name of the Church, with the intention which the Church attaches to them. They are the culminating events in the life of the Church. They are acts of faith which establish the Church. Now, the Church is the sacrament of Christ's constant presence in our midst and Christ himself, as God's incarnate Word, is the pre-eminent sacrament

4

—the "primordial sacrament" which bestows
a sacramental structure upon the whole of
the economy of salvation. By faith we encounter the risen Christ who is present in the
Church. By faith we come into communion
with him, come under the power of his word
and the influence of his spirit, are delivered
from our state of sinfulness and are made
partners in his resurrection. All this is made
possible, above all, by means of those public
acts of faith which we call the sacraments.
Professor Schillebeeckx has expressed it in
this way: "The sacraments of the Church are
not things. They are encounters between man
on earth and the man Jesus in glory."[1]

It is, of course, not my intention in this
book to go deeply into this new doctrine of
the sacraments,[2] but simply to direct the
reader's attention to two themes which seem

[1] See *Theologisch Woordenboek,* under "Sacrament", 3, col. 4202.

[2] For a more thorough exposition of this doctrine,
see, among others, E. Schillebeeckx, *De sacramentele
heilseconomie,* Antwerp (1952), and *Christ, the
Sacrament,* London and New York (1963); Dr P.
Anciaux, *Het sacrament der boetvaardigheid* and
Het sacrament van het huwelijk, Tielt and Lannoo
(1959); E. P. L. Monden, *Het Misoffer als mysterie,*
Roermond (1948).

to me to be of particular importance in connection with the layman's religious life.

THE SOCIAL CHARACTER OF THE SACRAMENTS

It is true that the sacraments have a direct bearing upon our personal salvation and demand our personal participation; they are in no way purely personal and private matters, since they bring about our salvation as members of the Church. They are, as we have already said, saving events which take place within the Church and which establish the Church, culminating events in the Church's life of faith and worship, acts which are fundamental to faith and worship. It is by means of these fundamental yet culminating acts that the Church establishes herself as a Church. It is through the sacraments that the Church comes into being as a Church, preserves herself as a Church and appears in the world as a Church. "As a Church" means here "as the visible and living dwelling-place of the invisible God", who, in word and spirit, lives among those who believe in him and gathers them together as "a kingly priesthood, a holy nation, God's own people". (1 Pet. 2.9.)

This vital aspect of the Church's sacraments is clearly discernible in each individual sacrament. It is above all apparent in the sacrament of baptism. It is with good reason that this sacrament has always been regarded by the Church as the basis of all the sacraments, since it is through baptism that we are received into the Church. We are called by baptism and given the power to take part in the Church's life of faith and worship as full members of the Church and to grow to full maturity in Christ. Baptism is the rite by which we are incorporated into the Church and thereby into Christ. It is, then, scarcely surprising that, in the ritual of baptism, the administration of the sacrament itself should form the climax of a dialogue with the faithful community: "Do you believe in God the Father almighty?" "I do believe." "Do you believe in Jesus Christ?" "I do believe." "Do you believe in the Holy Ghost?" "I do believe." "Are you willing to be baptized?" "I am willing." "I baptize thee in the name of the Father and of the Son and of the Holy Ghost." In this dialogue of faith, what takes place is, so to speak, a mutual agreement. Before the Christian community receives the new member and undertakes to watch over him and to allow him to take part in its life of worship, it requires of him a solemn confession of faith —"I do believe."

In the sacrament of confirmation, which is coming more and more to be regarded as the sacrament of maturity, this mutual agreement is renewed and strengthened (confirmed). The baptized Christian receives, in the sacrament, his mission and the grace to confess his faith with the whole of his personality, to bear heroic witness to this faith and to work and fight for it. From this time onwards, the Church entrusts him with responsibility.

It was not simply by chance that the sacrament of the Eucharist came to be known in common parlance as the "Blessed Sacrament". This sacrament is pre-eminent among the others, the culminating point of the sacramental life of the Church. Indeed, the celebration of the Eucharist occupies a special place among the many acts of public worship which take place in the Church. As the Lord's Supper, or *Coena Domini*, it is the act of worship in which the Church tries to express in the most perfect way, to show in the most sacred and visible manner and to realize in the most complete sense what she in fact is, in her inmost, invisible essence. This is, of

course, God's new people, established through
faith in Christ's death and resurrection into
a historical reality of which the head is the
risen Christ himself. The celebration of the
Eucharist is the gathering together of the
Christian community around the "Lord's
Table" for the purpose of commemorating
the death and resurrection of the Lord. But
it is more than this. It is also a "partaking of
the table of the Lord" (see 1 Cor. 10.21), an
eating of the "bread of God which cometh
down from heaven and giveth life to the
world" (John 6.33) and, finally, a giving of
thanks (*eucharistein*) to God, the source of
all life and the one who provides everything
for the sustenance of this life, the God whose
only Word "was made flesh and dwelt among
us" for our eternal salvation. It is, therefore,
not difficult to understand why this sacred
"Lord's Supper" came to be known, in the
early Church, as the "love-feast" of the faithful. (See 1 Cor. 11.21.) The word *agape*
(=love), which was used in this connection
had four meanings: God's love or the quality
of God's grace, the Christian's love of his
neighbour, the Church as a community of
love and finally the Holy Eucharist as the
sacrament of love. It would be difficult to find

a more striking demonstration than this of the pre-eminence of the Eucharist as a communal sacrament, a sacrament which presupposes and establishes the community.

It will, of course, be clear that no Christian who leads a sinful life can be admitted to the table of the Lord. "Whosoever shall eat this bread, or drink the chalice of the Lord unworthily, shall be guilty of the body and the blood of the Lord." (1 Cor. 11.27.) Before he can be re-admitted to the sacred mysteries of the love-feast, the sinner must bring about his return to God by means of an act of penance which is freely undertaken on his part and controlled by the Church. Hence the sacrament of penance, now commonly known as confession. This sacrament, too, is not a purely personal and private matter, and it is impossible to understand its full significance if it is not considered in association with the community of the Church. The word "confession" and the way in which this confession takes place nowadays—the idea of the "secret of the confessional" which is always connected with the sacrament—these have resulted in a false emphasis, in which the social character of the sacrament has become obscured. But, as we have already indicated, "confession"

was not the original name for the sacrament.
The original name was the "sacrament of
penance"—the sacrament, in other words, of
ecclesiastically and liturgically organized penance in which not only the sinner himself,
but also the entire Church was implicated.[1]
This social character is, of course, still present
in the present-day form of the ritual of confession, namely an ecclesiastical lawsuit
(hence the term "tribunal", or "court" of
confession and penance), followed by an
ecclesiastical verdict or judgement or, in the
normal language of the Church, an "absolution" which is pronounced by a priest possessing the necessary faculty, or "legal" power.

The sacraments of holy orders and of marriage have always been regarded as social
sacraments which enable the Church to exist
as such. We have already pointed out in the
preceding chapter that the Church, as the
new People of God, is inconceivable without
her sacred offices and functions which form
a meaningful whole and are now entrusted
to her priests. As far as the sacrament of
matrimony is concerned, this is nothing else
than the natural institution of marriage,

[1] The penitent used to be solemnly reconciled
with the Church on Maundy Thursday.

which was reinstated by Christ in its original wholeness and given a new meaning and a sacred function by virtue of the fact that it takes place within the Church.

For St Paul, marriage was a great mystery and a great sacrament, causing "a man to leave his father and mother" and to "cleave to his wife", so that they should be "two in one flesh". For him, the mystery was intimately related to Christ and his Church. (Eph. 5.31,32: "This is a great sacrament; but I speak in Christ and in the Church.") Marriage does not only symbolize the indissoluble bond of love existing between Christ and his bride, the Church. It is also a sharing in this love. Its significance goes even further, for marriage also implies a mission and a function within the Church. In the form of marital faithfulness and parental care, it has the task of bringing something of Christ's perfect and faithful love into the world and of bringing children too into the world and of educating them as the new People of God. In this way, every marriage which takes place in and for the Church acquires the significance and the validity of a sacrament of the Church. For this reason, the Council of Trent included matrimony among the seven sacraments.

Finally, no-one ought to find it in the least surprising that the Church as Church, that is, as the saving institution of Christ himself and the brotherhood of all Christians, should be present at the bedside of those of her members who are sick and dying, with her saving power, her prayer and her spiritual and physical help. The Epistle of St James informs us that this was the practice in the earliest Church: "Is any man sick among you? Let him bring in the priests of the church and let them pray over him, anointing him with oil in the name of the Lord. And the prayer of faith shall save the sick man. And the Lord shall raise him up. And if he be in sins, they shall be forgiven him." (James 5.14,15.) This, then, is the origin of the sacrament of the anointing of the sick, which, by the priest's unction and prayer can, according to the Catechism, lead to the salvation of those believers who are mortally sick. In this sacrament we see the last earthly encounter between the sick person and the risen Christ taking place. This encounter occurs through the Church—inclined for the last time towards her dying member and bringing to him her saving power, her prayer and all her attention, she is with him to the end. Even the purely secular medical attention which the sick man receives is included in the supernatural saving activity of Christ in this encounter and sanctified by it. This brings us to our second theme in connection with the new sacramental doctrine, which is of considerable importance for the layman today.

THE MEANING OF THE SACRAMENTS FOR THE LAYMAN IN HIS DAILY LIFE

It is precisely because the sacraments are saving events which take place within the Church and which establish and build up the Church—because they are culminating acts in the Church's life of faith and worship which form the community of the faithful—that they cannot be divorced from the normal, everyday life of the believer. The daily life of the laity is, so to speak, drawn into the divine order of salvation via the sacraments, and it would be quite wrong to limit their efficacy and their significance to the day or to the moment of their "reception". We are, however, always inclined to do this, though we may perhaps include the honeymoon in

the period of sacramental effectiveness in the
case of matrimony!

It is, however, particularly in the case of
baptism, confirmation and the ordination of
priests that we tend wrongly to limit the
meaning of the sacrament in this way, since
these sacraments set an ineffaceable "seal"
or "mark" upon the Christian's soul and con-
secrate him to God. Indeed, according to
most current interpretations, this "seal" or
mark, is really an irrevocable *sacra potestas*.
By this we mean a share in Christ's royal
priesthood and, following upon this, a lasting
power and mission in the service of God in
accordance with the Christian religion.[1] Baptism incorporates the believer for ever into
the "holy and priestly People of God". Confirmation calls him and empowers him to
confess his faith every day of his life and in
all the circumstances of his life and to be an
active witness on Christ's behalf. When a
Christian is ordained as a priest, he is called
to share in the pastoral office of the Lord and
is equipped with certain functions.[2]

[1] See St Thomas, *Summa Theol.*, 3, q. 63, a. 2;
4, q. 72, a. 5.
[2] See E. Schillebeeckx, in *Theologisch Woordenboek*, under "Sacrament", 3, col. 4224: "Every sign

Although there is no question of a "seal" being set on the soul in the case of marriage, there is nonetheless a definite and irrevocable *mission* in the Church implied in the sacrament. This mission not only includes the duty to procreate children for the new People of God. It also means that the partners in the Christian marriage have to bear a living testimony of a good family life and thereby show to the world that Christianity is a spiritual power causing "charity, joy and peace". (Gal. 5.22.) In other words, when we say that Christian marriage is a sacrament, what we mean is that the daily life of the partners, in their marriage and their family life, is included in the divine economy of salvation and in this sense possesses a sacramental aspect.

But the remaining three sacraments of penance, Holy Eucharist and the anointing of the sick, though they have no mission or function

___

or mark gives a specific mission of visible activity within the Church ... What is present in every baptized and confirmed member of the Church—the priestly messianism of the People of God—is also present in the priestly episcopate and, depending upon this, in the priesthood itself in the form of authority and leadership." See also E. J. De Smet, *Het priesterschap van de gelovigen*.

of this kind within the Christian community, should also never be seen in isolation from the normal life of the layman. If they are isolated in this way, there is a grave risk that much of their significance will be lost.

It is all too evident that the full content of the penitential aspect of the sacrament of penance is not brought into play by the perhaps rather humiliating confession of various sins and the short prayers or good works imposed by the confessor as a "penance" or satisfaction. Everything that is painful in human life is given a penitential significance in the rite of this sacrament, and the process of conversion, which forms an essential aspect of the Christian way of life and is never completed, is fully incorporated into it. That is why the priest says, after giving absolution: "May whatever good you have done, whatever evil you have suffered, gain for you a remission of your sins, an increase of grace, and the reward of eternal life."

Mutatis mutandis, the same can also be said of the Lord's Supper. It is equally applicable whether we regard it as the sacrament of thanksgiving (Eucharist), as the sacrament of brotherly love (*agape*) or as the sacrament of our participation in the sacrifice of the Cross (Mass). In this culminating event of the worship of the Church, the *whole* Christian is drawn into the sacred action and his whole life finds expression in it at the deepest level which is, of course, religious.

What happens in the Eucharist, considered as the sacrament of thanksgiving, is that homage is paid to God for the great gift of life and everything which sustains this life: "The eyes of all hope in thee, O Lord; and thou givest them meat in due season." (Ps. 144.15; this passage occurs in the Gradual of the Feast of Corpus Christi.) This food has as many aspects as life itself. There is the daily bread which preserves our life in the biological sense and is the basic condition for all life on earth. There is also the bread of the civilized society that feeds the spirit of man, for "man does not live by bread alone". But above all there is the bread that is Jesus himself, the bread which, as the Word of God, has come down to us from heaven to enable us to share in the divine life. It is for all this that we pay homage and give thanks to God in the celebration of the Eucharist, to God the Father, from whom all good things proceed. It is for all this, too, that we bear witness before the world that God is the beginning

and the end of all life and that we may with
trust and gratitude look life in the face whatever the circumstances of our life may be,
because this life comes from God and leads
us back to God: "I believe in the life ever-
lasting."

Let us now consider briefly this dimension
of the sacrament in its sacrificial aspect. When
we gather round the "Lord's Table", for the
purpose of commemorating his death and resurrection, we must not simply unite ourselves in spirit with the Lord's death on the
Cross, but, proceeding from the Mass, build
up and extend our daily lives into a "living
sacrifice, holy and pleasing unto God". (Rom.
12.1.) In all the varying circumstances and
vicissitudes of our lives we should, consequently, be able to preserve that attitude of
mind with which Christ was imbued, so that
he was able to "humble himself, becoming
obedient unto death, even to the death of the
cross". (Phil. 2.8.)

This attitude of mind, however, which was
Christ's on the Cross and which we must assimilate into our own lives, does not only mean
that we should surrender completely to God's
will, but also that we should give ourselves
to our brothers in brotherly love: "Greater

love than this no man hath, that he lay down his life for his friends." (John 15.13.) We must be mindful of this too, and assimilate it into our own lives in the eucharistic "Lord's Supper" which has been called *agape* for this reason. In this context, St Paul's admonition is strictly pertinent: "When you come, therefore, together in one place, it is not now to eat the Lord's supper. For every one taketh before his own supper to eat. And one indeed is hungry and another is drunk." (1 Cor. 11.20–21.) It is, of course, true that, in the celebration of the Eucharist today, the sacramental commemoration of the Last Supper is completely distinct from the eating of any ordinary meal. This does not, however, mean that the Eucharist is in any way deprived of its sacramental aspect of brotherly love or *agape*. As a result, we are not worthy to sit at the Lord's Table if the love-feast of the Lord does not bring us closer to our fellow men justice in day-to-day relationships with others. If we thank God for the grace of life and the If we thank God for the grace of life and the food which he provides for the physical, mental and spiritual sustenance of this life and yet refuse to give anything ourselves to our starving neighbour, we can scarcely claim to be pleasing God.

As we have already pointed out, even the anointing of the sick has a bearing upon our everyday life. The anointing of the sick is the sacrament of the Church's concern for her suffering and dying members, both in the physical and in the spiritual sense. These two aspects of the care of the sick are inseparably united, especially in the rite of anointing, and particularly when medical attention has been unsuccessful. The fact that the doctor's and the priest's functions are now separate does not mean that they are entirely unrelated to each other. The sacrament of the anointing of the sick is a constant reminder to us that the purely medical care of the sick has a religious significance within the Christian community.

What conclusion may we draw from all this? One certain conclusion is that a greater awareness of the sacramental structure of the Christian economy of salvation is of the utmost importance for the laity. For a long time now the laity has been pressing for a more active share in the sacramental and liturgical life of the Church. The problem of how this can be achieved, however, cannot be separated from another, and perhaps more important question—how can the daily life of the laity be drawn into the Church's sacramental life, inspired and sanctified by it, so that this lay life itself can become a visible sign and testimony of the invisible and divine aspect of the Christian life of faith? For it is only then that the lives of the faithful will take on the full meaning of the Good News.

For this to come about, two things are necessary. The first requirement is a more thorough liturgical education, by means of which the Christian laity will be led to a deeper understanding of the true meaning of the sacraments. The second need is for a more careful presentation of the Liturgy itself, a liturgy which better expresses the nature of the sacramental acts and rites and whose visible form corresponds far more closely to the invisible realities of salvation it incorporates.[1]

THE ESSENCE OF THE LAY APOSTOLATE

The word "apostolate" comes from the Greek *apostolos*, meaning a messenger, envoy

[1] See "Voor een levende liturgie", *Universitas-tijdschrift*, Antwerp (1954).

or ambassador. Christianity is itself God's joyous message. The apostolate, then, is not something which is incidental to Christianity. It is an essential part of it.

What we have to say here about the lay apostolate is directly related to our brief outline of the place and function of the Church in the order of salvation in the first chapter. It is only if the lay apostolate is seen in the light of the ideas developed in that chapter that full justice can be done to it. As we said there, God is not a magical power, but a *living God* who accomplishes the eternal salvation of the human race by means of his Word and his Spirit. The sovereign power of God's gracious condescension in the accomplishment of this salvation at the same time includes man's free co-operation. There is no question here of a causality in the third Person. What happens is rather an encounter between God and the whole of the human race through the agency of men situated within concrete, historical contexts. In the Old Testament, we find that Israel's contact with God takes place through her great men of God. The New-Testament parallel is to be found in Jesus Christ, the incarnate Word of God, and the new Israel or the Church. This explains the essential role of the Church in the mystery of salvation. In other words, Christianity, in the sense of the "mystery of the Word", or God's work of salvation through his Word and Spirit, cannot be divorced from Christianity, in the sense of the "ministry of the Word", or the proclamation and service of that Word. As St Paul says in the much-quoted passage from his Epistle to the Romans, the Christian message is the "power of God unto salvation to every one that believeth in it". (Rom. 1.16.) This means that wherever the Christian message is proclaimed by word and by example, God is *present* in that place with his Word and his Spirit. That is why we have been able to define the Church, the vehicle of this message, as the holy place on earth where God lives and works and as the "Bride of the Lord"— God's partner and witness. The Church, as the living society of the faithful, priests and laymen, is essentially a missionizing, evangelizing and catechizing community. In a word, it is an apostolic community, in the service of the divine message which is directed to the whole world via the Church.

The layman is consequently called to an apostolate. He is not called to be an indirect apostle, acting through the agency of the Church's priests and merely serving to assist the priests in this task. He is, by virtue of his baptism and his membership of the Church, called to a direct apostolate. As Pope Pius XII once observed, "Lay men and women must become increasingly aware of the fact that they do not simply belong to the Church. They are the Church."[1] In everything that they do and say, in the day-to-day witness of their lives and the Christian practice of their lay vocations, the lay people of the Church co-operate in the *aedificatio Ecclesiae*, the building up of the Church into a "sign of God among the nations". As I have already observed in *Geloof en Wereld*,[2] without the sanctity of her members and their faithfulness to the Gospel, the Church would hardly be able to appear in the world as the faithful Bride of the Word and a holy temple of God built up of living stones, where the Father is worshipped "in spirit and in truth". (John 4.23.) She would not, moreover, appear as the place of light and peace to the pilgrim in search of God.

Faith and the apostolate are, therefore,

[1] Address to the Cardinals, 20 February 1946.
[2] pp. 51–2.

intimately related to each other. Faith which lacks an apostolic orientation is no true faith. The apostolate which is not firmly rooted in faith can never bear fruit. Faith is much more than the possession of speculative knowledge. It is a question of being at all times at God's disposal, of being available to undertake one's share in his saving work. This readiness on our part finds its expression in our prayer, which is an opening of the mind to God's Word and the activity of his Spirit, and is brought to perfection in our apostolate by being translated into service and work. Prayer and the apostolate—these are really two aspects of the same act of faith, two ways of showing our trust in God and of entering into God's plan for the salvation of mankind. By prayer and the apostolate, we can make God's creative and sanctifying will the fundamental inspiration of our existence: "Thy kingdom come; thy will be done on earth." Our entire apostolate must be carried out in faith and as a result of faith. It must be, as it were, born of prayer. What is bound to emerge from the foregoing is, then, that the apostolate is in no way the monopoly of the priest, but is an essential part of every truly religious life.

The idea that every Christian is, by virtue

of his baptism and his reception into the
Church, called to an apostolate is as old as
Christianity itself. If we are more aware of it
now than ever before, it is because it is an
idea of decisive importance for the future of
the Church, in view of the religious situation
of Christianity today in the world. The uni-
fication of the world, increasing seculariza-
tion in temporal affairs, frequent contact between different peoples and societies in a
spirit of positive toleration, growing pressure
towards social emancipation, the rise of a new
kind of atheism with a humanistic slant—all
these aspects of a changing society show
clearly how urgent and indispensable the layman's part is in the spread of the Faith today.
Those days are past when the spread of Christianity, the coming of Western civilization
and the establishment of political power
formed a single, indivisible whole. There is
only one thing which will from now on ap-
peal to men, both at home and in the mission
countries, and prepare the way for Christ's
Church, and that is the radiant witness of the
Christian way of life which appears to men as
a liberating message which is firmly rooted
in divine grace. In this present age, more than
ever before, the truth of the Gospel statement

is borne out: "By the fruit the tree is known." (Matt. 12.33.)

Forms of the Lay Apostolate

It is, of course, obvious that the layman's contribution towards the spread of the Faith, the extension of the Church and the flourishing of the Church's life can take many different forms.

In the first place, there is a form of contribution which is directly and primarily religious, but which is also basically of the same order as, and a continuation of, the religious mission of the Church and her hierarchy. Examples of this are active lay participation in the Church's liturgical life, pastoral work within the parish, religious instruction and participation in various kinds of educative movements and activities and, last but by no means least, the daily witness of a Christian life.

It is, however, also possible for the layman to serve his faith and work towards its spread in an indirect way. He can do this by co-operating in the building up of a secular world which respects Christian views and gives the Church the freedom and space she needs in order to accomplish her task. The apostolic layman will, then, be involved in the sciences, economics, politics, the Press, teaching, and in every kind of lay profession. As these are activities whose object is secular, they do not come under the direct authority of the Church's hierarchy. That their beneficial effect on the religious life is only indirect does not imply that they are of purely secondary importance. They can have a decisive influence upon the success or the eclipse of the Church in certain parts of the world and under certain circumstances.

As far as the term "Catholic Action" is concerned, it need hardly be stressed that the phrase is extremely elastic, and may be applied to all kinds of religious and secular Catholic actions and activities. It is quite probable that the term "Catholic Action" had this broad meaning in some of the pronouncements and writings of Pope Pius XII. Now, however, "Catholic Action" is generally used to denote that aspect of the lay apostolate which is hierarchically organized, that is to say, an apostolate which is primarily religious, takes the form of an organized movement and is under the direct authority of the Hierarchy. In this narrower sense, Catholic Action is simply one of the many possible forms of the lay apostolate. It would, therefore, be a dangerous mistake to identify the entire lay apostolate with Catholic Action, and thereby perhaps give the impression that everything that happens outside Catholic activity organized or led by the clergy is not an authentic apostolate. If this is done, there is a grave danger that Catholic Action, instead of helping the laity to achieve a mature status, may lead to a new kind of clericalism. The result might well be a harmful division in the ranks of the faithful, an organizational despotism and a complete stifling of that apostolate which is of such great importance today—the apostolate of the intellect and of the intellectual.

CONCLUSION: THE APOSTOLATE OF THE INTELLECT

B Y "apostolate of the intellect" I mean
an attitude of mind which is honest,
impartial and open to the truth, wherever this truth may come from, and which is
at the same time deeply concerned with free,
critical speculation, arising from a "love of
the truth and nothing but the truth". (Cardinal Mercier.)

Free, critical thought,[1] without which no
judicious and justified understanding of the
truth can ever be reached in any department
of human activity, is pre-eminently the task
of the intellectual, and particularly the uni-
versity-trained intellectual. This is his irre-
placeable function in society. It is only by
intellectual awareness that society can be

---

[1] It should be remembered that all true thought
is both free and critical. It is not "free" in the sense
that it leads to a complete absence of discipline and
a state of anarchy, but in the sense that it is subject
only to the pure truth. The word "critical" must
also be taken here in its original meaning. In the
sense of the Greek *krinein*, it means to distinguish
between truth and untruth, between worth and
worthlessness.

protected from mental conservatism and rigidity and from the depersonalizing effects of the absolute power of organization in our world.

This is not to say that society should be entirely without organization and authority. What I mean is that organized society has need of free, independent thought if it is not to die of a morbid hardening of the arteries. Organization and intellect are complementary powers within society. It is only within the tension that exists between the two poles that society can lead a healthy life. This is true not only of temporal society, but also of religious society, the Church. There is a place in the Church too for a specifically intellectual apostolate and therefore a place for the intellectual, be he priest or layman, scientist, philosopher or theologian.

The Church has never been able to do without this apostolate of the intellect. It is itself implied in the idea of message. Whenever we think of the word "message" the words "conversation", "dialogue", "witness" and "word" itself come at once to mind and consequently "understanding"—understanding for the person to whom this word is addressed. Force, social pressure and prestige do not belong to the idea of message, above all to the Christian message. It is only in free dialogue, conducted at the level of mutual understanding and respect, that the word of the message can strike home with all its liberating power.[1]

This is, of course, particularly so in the case of dialogue between partners who are no longer children, but mature human beings and lovers of freedom. As I have already tried to show in my analysis of the modern world in *Geloof en Wereld*, this is, when all is said and done, the greatest event of our times. Mankind has put away the things of a child and, to quote Karl Jaspers, has "lost its naïvety". This accounts for the enormous importance for Christianity today of honest, open dialogue with all men, dialogue which is full of respect for, understanding of and receptivity towards everything that appeals to and intimately affects humanity now. The words of the Evangelist, "The truth shall make you free" (John 8.32), may be understood in this sense as well. It is only a great openness to the truth, wherever this truth may come from and wherever it is to be

[1] We should not forget, of course, that all living witness is a form of dialogue.

found, that will make Christianity free today
and give Christianity the full power of its
liberating message. The preservation of this
open-minded attitude towards the truth, in
the realization that we shall never be finished
with the truth and that no-one can presume
to a monopoly of the whole truth, is above
all the task of the intellectual. The Church
has perhaps never before in her history had
such need of the apostolate of the intellect
as now, when the world is rapidly becoming
one and every value is being questioned.
Finally, I must emphasize that, in the apostolate of the intellect, I include every aspect of
intellectual life—scientific research, social
and political thought, literary creation, true
philosophy and, above all, theology allied to
contemporary thought and the language of
today.